JOURNEY
Through the Valley of the
GIANTS

L.J. LONG

© Copyright 2020 by L.J.Long, LLC

All rights reserved.

No part of this book may be reproduced by any mechanical, photographic, or electronic process, or in the form of phonographic recording, nor may it be stored in a retrieval system, transmitted, or otherwise copied for public or private use, without written permission from the author.

Bible scriptures quoted from the *New American Standard Bible* (NASB).

For information about 7 Rivers Revitalization Group, Inc., visit:
www.sevenriversrgi.com

L.J.Long, LLC
Journeywithljlong@gmail.com
www.lisajlong.net

Printed in the United States of America
Published October 2020

Book Design & Layout: Maria Robinson, Designs On You, LLC
www.designsonyou.weebly.com
Original Cover Concept Drawing: Daniel J. Long
Colorized Adaptation of Cover Illustration: Jeff Williamson, www.jwdx.co
Drawings: pages 18, 105, 108: Daniel J. Long

ISBN paperback: 9781735534503
ISBN ebook: 9781735534510

dedication

To my Lord and Savior, Christ Jesus.

And to His faithful servant, T.D. Jakes.

acknowledgments

WITH GRATITUDE TO...

- *my Lord, Jesus*—eternal praises and thanksgiving, for You deserve all the Glory.

- *my mom, Janice*—for her love and for always speaking words of encouragement at the right time.

- *my friend, Chris*—for always listening and being the shoulder I leaned on while lamenting my journey through the valley.

- *my prayer partners*—for driving hundreds of miles to ensure I was prayed over during a critical moment during my life-saving surgery.

- *my sisters*—for their countless hours of support and for putting out requests for prayer from the multitude when I needed it most.

- *my son*—for bravely confronting his fears and for his desire to care for me.

- *my employer and co-workers*—who never gave up on me and ensured I always had a place to be welcome.

- *my art director, graphic designer and editor, Maria*—for her discernment, staying the course, and having the desire to ensure this message was published.

- *my brother and creative artist, Dan*—thank you; do what I say —bidden 100.

- *the illustrator of the book cover, Jeff*—for your desire to create and make it come alive!

from the author

I walked as a Christian for twenty years before my journey through the Valley of the Giants. I was twenty-three when I was water baptized and received Jesus Christ as my Lord and Savior on March 16, 1991.

For the next ten years, I did nothing but break every commandment. Then I came face-to-face with the end of myself. I realized the laws I kept for myself were, in fact, the very things killing me.

By that time I was married and my son, Bradley, was one year old. He was in my arms that day when I felt myself going down. I gently put him in his crib, sat on the edge of my bed, and screamed, I hate myself!

Silence. Everything stopped.

I'd never had such a thought, never hated myself. I was a performance-driven person. I knew that much. I had a strong desire for working hard and wanted to outdo myself in everything I touched. That wasn't something I did with conscious intent, but something I came to understand about myself later. I was competitive and did everything I could to avoid making mistakes. I took on extra things and did everything myself because I didn't want to be disappointed. I didn't understand how to communicate my expectations to others in a healthy way for them or for me, so I avoided all kinds of confrontation.

I was ten years into my Walk With Jesus but I never could measure up. I could never have a good day just being with myself. I could no longer meet my own expectations for what my mind was telling me I had to have in order to be okay.

Sitting on the edge of my bed that day, having a meltdown, I prayed. Lord, I don't know anything anymore but I do know that you are my God. Come and get me.

Nothing happened. So, I waited. And waited. Two months later, I was standing at the kitchen sink washing dishes in our little trailer home when the voice of Satan showed up. *HE IS NOT COMING*. With a stern voice I replied—OH YES, HE IS—and I kept washing dishes. He left.

Three more uneventful months went by.

Then the phone rang. A good friend asked if I wanted to join a Bible study. I jumped at the chance! My "new" Walk had finally commenced! That five-month waiting period reminds me of when Daniel prayed and fasted earnestly for twenty-one days, waiting for God's answer. And when an angel of the Lord appeared to Daniel, the angelic messenger said that God had heard the first of his prayers, but that he (the angel) had been opposed those twenty-one days by the prince of Persia. (Daniel 10:12-13)

During the next two years, I pursued the Lord diligently and He answered every prayer, every time. I came to a place in my studies where I kept hearing, *Know who you are in Christ.* I went home from the Sunday class I attended one day and asked the Lord—What does it mean to "Know who you are in Christ?" Out of the blue, the instructor of my Sunday class mailed the book *Classic Christianity* to me. While reading the book in my living room chair, I came to a quotation from 1 Corinthians 3:16. *Do you not know that you are the temple of God and that the Spirit of God dwells in you?*

When I read those Words, I came Alive! I felt like I'd been hit with lightning or fire. My body was electrified. I had been baptized in the Holy Spirit! In that moment I could feel my flesh over my spirit. I didn't know what to do but figured I was supposed to get used to it. I wasn't going to be rid of my body. I had to keep living. For three days after that I felt like my feet weren't touching the ground and I was walking on air.

I later moved to the Reservation with my husband and son and spent three years in the "Desert" meditating on the Word of God, renewing my mind.

The Holy Spirit tested me with acts of giving, forgiveness and applying the Word. I was called into service, cast off spirits, attacked by an unclean spirit, sought out to lead prayer groups for the terminally ill, gifted a car. When I walked into rooms, strangers handed newborn babies to me and asked for a blessing. The list goes on…. Glory be to God alone!

I never thought I would go to another level of understanding in the Lord. I distinctly remember begging God to not take me through another season of renewing the mind. During that period in the Desert, I felt painful changes occur in my brain. I even went through a time when my equilibrium was completely off. The ground would rise up and hit me in the face to change the thoughts that needed changing. What was happening? I went to a neurologist and electrodes were hooked up to my head. No explanation was found for these physical complications.

Then one day God said, *It's time to engage.* So I figured my training was done and I was where I was supposed to be in the Lord; that this was my measure of faith. And now I would just be on a journey, going through events and circumstances, doing the work of the Lord until it was time to go home.

My calling included planting seeds, ministry work (helps) and exercising my gifts in the Spirit. Gifts of intercession, exhortation (comfort), discernment and counseling. These were the areas where I believed I flourished and produced the most fruit for the Lord.

My Desert time had given me the ability to let things go and to shift my way of thinking. My understanding of the world and how I interpreted events was completely different. I would not and could not have predicted yet another level of renewing my mind. Much different from my time in the Desert, the Valley was next.

contents

dedication iii
acknowledgements v
from the author vii

1   Breaking the Foundation 1
2   Transition 13
3   Giant with Aftershocks 15
4   Fighting the Same Giant 19
5   Hope in the Valley 23
6   Battle After Battle 27
7   Giant After Giant 35
8   The Testing of Giants 41

9	Breakthrough	43
10	False Hope Giant	47
11	Kidnapper Giant	51
12	The Giant Miracle	55
13	Intensive Care	59
14	Aging Giant	79
15	Suicide Giant	85
16	Bankruptcy Giant	89
17	Light in the Valley	91
18	Coming Through the Other Side	95
19	Gifts from Above	99
20	Rebuilding the Foundation	103

epilogue: Living with Giants—The Journey Continues ... 107

about the author 108

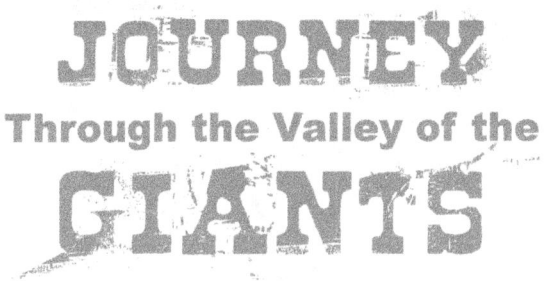

No matter what kind of giant you're facing,
God will get you through it.

L.J. LONG

CHAPTER 1

BREAKING THE FOUNDATION

It was during the year 2010 when I moved from working in one ministry to another. Among other duties in the first ministry, I was a social services representative to a Coalition. The Coalition was formed from a minimum of thirty social service agencies and local nonprofits, and was tasked with addressing the initiative to reduce the prison recidivism rate in our state.

After some time, the Coalition was set to apply for a grant to implement a new prison re-entry program. The program called for hiring a Coordinator for each pilot site. I distinctly remember, during a Coalition meeting, that the Holy Spirit moved me to apply for the Coordinator job. I went back to my office and told my boss that if the Coalition runs for this grant with the State, I would apply for the Coordinator position. He said, "Okay," and made no attempt to change my mind or keep me in the ministry I was currently working in.

So, when the grant was awarded, I applied for the job with the city and went through the interviews. I was beat out by just one person. Her husband happened to be the current Fire Chief of the city. When that happened I thought, Lord, what is going on? You told me to apply for this job, and here I am, and I'm not getting the job!

The Holy Spirit spoke to me saying, *Two months*. Two months? What does that mean? What's going to happen in two months? The Holy Spirit spoke again: *Two months*. Okay, okay, I thought.

I continued to work and wait as the two months passed. I continued to attend the re-entry program meetings as my ministry's representative, and I observed the Coordinator in her new position. I felt challenged with deciding how I would interact with her and how I would treat her. I remember wanting to feel stubborn, selfish and resentful about losing. I wanted to let her figure out the position on her own.

I was being tested. The Holy Spirit revealed a crossroads in my thoughts: You can either help this person or throw her under the bus. How would you want to be treated? So, I made the choice to welcome her, bless her and pray for her instead of being resentful. I was courteous and offered my help to her so she could do her job better and feel genuinely received. I felt the difference in myself and the shift from the Holy Spirit when I had done this. It felt good.

I was always second guessing everything, but within the two months her spouse took a different job in a distant city and state. She put in her notice to leave the Coordinator position. I was just floored, and once again, God had shown me His faithfulness.

It was the spring of 2010. The city called and I was offered the Coordinator job. So, I left the ministry where I was working to be the coordinator for the city's new prison re-entry program. But before I left, a wonderful group of women staff gave gifts to me and wished me well. A key staff member who didn't want me to leave asked if my boss had offered anything to me to stay. Nope. That one conversation reinforced long-held feelings of resentment and foundational thoughts I still had of needing to be rescued and loved.

During the time I worked for the city as the Coordinator I was stretched. I learned an amazing number of new things and did what I thought I wasn't capable of doing. Seven months passed.

A Board of Directors member from my previous ministry position asked me to lunch. I went, and during our meal she asked me to come back and become their Executive Director (ED). My first response to her was, Does the current ED (Tom) know this? She said, "Yes, he's leaving." I was challenged by this response because I knew Tom had been trying to leave for years. I never could figure out if It was a game he played for his ego, or if he was wrestling with God. I said to her, "Let me think and pray about this and then I will give you an answer." We finished our lunch and I returned to my office.

I labored in prayer. I prayed and prayed for two months, and still I did not get a definitive answer one way or the other. However, what I did get was, *You will be blessed no matter which you do. God is with you.* I can tell you, at the time my response to God was, Well THAT doesn't help me! Wrong attitude, right? In my mind I could see both the challenge of going back to the previous ministry or staying with my Coordinator job. I was looking for the easy way.

Finally, I agreed to apply for the ED position. I went through an initial interview process where I met with the board and discussed my qualities and capabilities. It was December 2010 when I accepted the ED job. The boss I had with the Coordinator position for the city that I was leaving sat in my office and cried. She told me she had just gotten off the phone with Tom and, in so many words, let me know I was being tricked into coming back. I remember looking at her and told her it was okay.

Shortly after, I was informed in a private meeting with Tom that I would never become the ED. I would just be the Assistant ED. The board would not allow a woman to be ED. I felt deceived but knew that this was how he operated to get what he wanted. It always seemed like a game with him and I knew that before I went back. But it is God who I serve, so I stayed on as the Assistant ED.

During the first month as the Assistant ED, the board member who asked me to lunch that day and offered the ED job to me resigned from the ministry. During the first six months in 2011, the Board of Directors moved forward with searching for a new ED. I distinctly remember in one board meeting that a lead member turned and looked at me and said: "So, how does all this make you feel?" I humbled myself and just said, "I will do what is asked of me. If that means I am the Assistant ED to a new ED, then that is what I will do." I knew the ministry well and I didn't want to leave. I wanted to serve my Lord.

I would be lying if I didn't tell you I silently struggled to accept it, though. At the time, I had always hoped one of the other board members would confront Tom. Someone with leverage. But *he* was the one with all the leverage! He had the personality and ability to influence many others, and he did. He knew most of the people who held positions of authority in the community. He could easily ruin reputations or get the respect of other leaders. I think his influence was their deterrent.

Now it was the summertime of 2011. The newly hired ED only stayed three weeks after accepting the position. There had been a huge flood in the location he was transitioning from, and he still held the leadership position of that ministerial region. He quickly decided to resign and not try to take on two ministries during this disastrous situation. The flood took precedence.

As the fall season approached, the Board of Directors asked me to become the new ED at the beginning of 2012. I accepted. This was a tough balance for me. I understood the pressures of the job and I knew I would only last three years. Five tops. Well, I assumed that was how long I would be in the position. I knew the president didn't approve of women in leadership roles. So I had to win him over. The only opportunity to spend quality time in his presence was during a strategic planning session the board was holding before the beginning of the new year. There was a need to implement a new, larger kitchen for the increased number of people the ministry served…a big renovation project. That was the only time I ever got positive feedback and comments of support from him. I thought that was a good sign.

The annual budget for 2012 was also to be completed soon...a daunting task since the figures for grants had not been handled correctly in previous budgets. In addition, Tom was trying to make budget cuts *for* me by suggesting I lay off female staff members who had been in the ministry for fifteen years. I knew what the end result would be, and I didn't take the bait. Then, over a meal one day, he admitted that he hates women. I often wonder what my face looked like because the next thing he said was that it was a mistake to have told that to me.

Finally, after working for several weeks on the budget, back-and-forthing with the board president for approval, I was almost finished. But it wasn't soon enough for the president. Next thing I know he's yelling at me in an email to finish the budget, punctuated with bold type, all caps and exclamation marks. I mumbled to myself, Are you *seriously* yelling at me in an email? As far as I remember, the budget has *never* been finished before the new calendar year had begun. So why should this year be any different?

I was wedged in an absurd predicament. I knew I needed to revamp the budget so I could hire more help, but I was out of time. And just like before, Tom had never really moved on. He had drawn up a contract conveniently making himself an irreversible consultant to provide support and carry on the Foundation's work. (The Foundation was a newly created trust fund to raise money for the long-term sustainability of the ministry). As a result, he designated a good share of the salary he had been making as a full-time employee of the ministry to himself. At the time, he'd convinced me not to promote anyone to Assistant ED for political reasons. When I look back on it, I realize his strategy was to make sure the budget's bottom line would not change and thereby accommodate his new contracted salary.

Now I was performing the work of at least four positions: Executive Director, Assistant Executive Director, Human Resources Director, and Fundraising Director. Now I was the one who wrote all the grant applications, and a third of the budget was derived from government grants.

At the time, I believed that if I asked for the help I needed, it would be used against me and I would be accused of incompetence. So, being the performance driven person I was, I decided it was just easier for me to work harder. I dealt with the budget I had.

After three months in the ED position, I finally received a Job Description. Two more months later, I was called to an evaluation and advised I was still in a probationary period. Tom attempted to control the Board of Directors by providing a template for my evaluation. The board didn't accept it. Since he couldn't control the board's evaluation of me, he tried a different tactic. He built resentment against me by talking poorly about me to my staff. Even one of my most prophetic friends who worked in the ministry made condemning remarks to me. I was so disappointed with people's lack of insight and discernment, especially those who had been baptized in the Holy Spirit.

Instead of confronting them about how I felt, I went before the Lord and asked, Would you talk to them about what is happening to me?!

Later, some of them would came up to me and said, "Oh, when I was in prayer, God showed me that you were being pressed down really hard, like in a pressing machine." But no apology would come. I think that most of us don't think about what we say to people or think about its impact before we speak. Including me.

It was June 2012 when my performance evaluation was finally delivered. The board apologized for their delay and graded me as insufficient in most every aspect of the position. Their biggest issue was a complaint they received from my former boss at the city. Remember the one who sat in my office, concerned for me and crying, that I was being tricked into leaving the job I had with her? Her grievance was about an email I'd sent to one of her staff. I was upset and criticized her for not getting information to me that I needed for a grant deadline. The board president said the city was offended and that my email was unbecoming of an ED. He also emphasized this incident was something that could cost our organization its funding. The board claimed it had seen "the email" and quickly moved to a corrective action plan for my employment. I was not given an opportunity to address the complaint. I didn't think I had a right to say, *Yes*, let's *do* look at "the email."

The evaluation took place during the month we were preparing for the kitchen renovation project. At the same time, we held public bidding for construction, relocated the displaced kitchen, tried to feed 500 homeless community members daily, organized building inspections for government grants, addressed an assault on a female staff member, and, to top it off, one of our homeless guests started a fire at one of our other facilities. (The ministry had five separate facilities throughout the city implementing seven different programs.)

So, yes, I was frustrated when I sent "the email." I can honestly say I don't recall punctuating it with outrageous language, bold face, all caps and exclamation marks. However, I'm sure my words were chastising because I was about to miss her deadline because of her own inaction. And instead of speaking with me directly, she fired back by calling our board president. I remember sitting in my office, crying and explaining all this to Tom. He was sympathetic at the time and said, Tell me what to do. But I had nothing. There was nothing I could ask him to do that would take it all back or take away the course of action that was already set in motion.

It didn't matter anyway. This was all the board president

needed to get rid of a woman in a leadership position he felt didn't belong there in the first place.

In June of 2012, the board put me on a corrective action plan for sixty days. The goals they set were literally impossible for anyone to achieve, but I tried anyway. For the next two months I did my best to raise and leverage as much money as I could, increase donor retention, deal with all the other areas they said were deficient, plus run Operations. I documented all my work, but about forty-five days into it I realized it was useless. I could feel myself starting to physically crack from the pressure. At that point I decided it wasn't worth losing myself and mentally threw in the towel. My fight was over. I felt the extreme, intense burden of pressure begin to release. But I still had to go through the sixty-day follow-up meeting with the Board of Directors committee assigned to my evaluation.

The day had come. It was a warm evening in August. I pulled up in my car to the Foundation's office, ready with my stack of papers to prove my work. When I got into the Board Room, I laid the stack on the table. After informing the committee I'd done all I could, the board president turned to me and said he trusted my word on what I'd accomplished, but he proceeded with the firing process anyway. He reviewed the evaluation documents and didn't even address any of my work. The board said it would accept my letter of resignation or I would face termination. They demanded to have my decision by Friday. I silently wept as we all left the room that evening. This was **The first Giant in the Valley.**

Perhaps you're reading this and thinking: So what? That's *nothing*. You should see what *I've* been through!

For me, it was huge. I had never been in the crossfire of a political battle. I had never been laid off, terminated, fired, chewed out or written up since entering the workforce at age fourteen. Ever. It was a big deal to me. I always wanted to do the right thing. Little did I know, this was just the leading edge of the Valley.

CHAPTER 2

TRANSITION

I went home after leaving the Foundation's office that August night. Later the same evening I got a call from the emergency room at the local hospital asking if I knew Paul. I said I did. (I'd had an on and off again relationship with Paul for a few years.) The ER attendant said Paul had been beaten with a bat and suffered a broken back.

I rounded the corner of the pod in the ER at the same time a security officer was reaching into Paul's room to shut off the lights, an attempt to calm him. When the officer saw me coming he motioned, questioning if I was going into the room. Good thing I arrived just in time. Paul had severe PTSD from being in prison previously, and shutting off the lights would have flipped him out, the opposite effect than what they were trying to accomplish.

I went in, sat down and watched him as he lay there. Because he was so intoxicated, he was having hallucinations and talking to his deceased father. When he called out loudly, I told him to be quiet. It was kinda funny because after arguing with the phantom of his father for awhile, he finally recognized my voice and calmed down. He tried to get up and leave, which was *not* going to happen with a broken back. I told him to shut up, lay down, and comply with the doctors. He did what I asked. I left later that night when they took him for x-rays of his head and back.

The next morning I wrote my letter of resignation and delegated projects and important documents to my right-hand staff. I made arrangements for everything I was working on, including packing up personal items in my office. Two members of the executive board came to my office that Friday to officially relieve me of my position, so I handed over the keys and walked straight out. I felt the Holy Spirit release me and felt like dancing right out the door! That afternoon I finished with a call to Tom, told him my decision, and that "it" was all his again.

CHAPTER

3

GIANT WITH AFTERSHOCKS

I'd met Paul the summer of 2008 during the time I was separated from my husband. The tidal wave I felt after meeting Paul swept me up and made it that much easier for the enemy to use him against me. And at that point, I didn't care.

I'd been waiting for my husband to fight for our marriage but he didn't. He let me deliver on all the threats I'd made. I gave him ultimatums to get help with the consequence of divorce if he didn't. The day he left I asked him if we were worth fighting for. He said: *We'll see.*

I turned around and walked out of the room as he left our home. I was devastated. I remember thinking—I'm not worth fighting for? Your son and I are not worth fighting for?! Then don't let the door hit you on your way out!

I really needed HIM to fight for us because I didn't have the strength anymore. I proceeded with filing for legal separation, and later, for divorce. **The Giant with Aftershocks.**

For a couple of weeks after Paul's hospitalization, he recuperated in the public hospital and it came time for his discharge. I made the mistake of agreeing to take him into my care, so the hospital released him to me instead of a nursing home or rehab facility. After his release I drove him around to pick up the medical supplies he would need from Health Services. Since it was a Saturday, the Social Service office was closed at the hospital and we were told to come back Monday when their main office would be open.

It was impossible for me to move Paul from the vehicle into my house without a walker. He was a big man and there was no way I could move him without some effort from him. It was then that I realized what I'd done to myself, and what the system had done to me. As medical professionals they knew darn well what I was about to deal with, but they didn't want to "waste" more time (read money) on his care. So, I went to the local department store to purchase several physical disability items or else he'd have been stuck in my vehicle for days!

Paul stayed with me for only a couple weeks before we ended up in an argument, and that gave him the excuse to leave he'd been looking for. During those two weeks, I'd thought that if I purchased several art supplies for him and took care of his needs, that would nourish his feelings of self worth. He was an amazing artist and a passionate person, and I was truly consumed with him. When he was sober. I'd never met anybody like him, but his mental health issues were just too much for me. He was **The Giant that Kept Coming Back.**

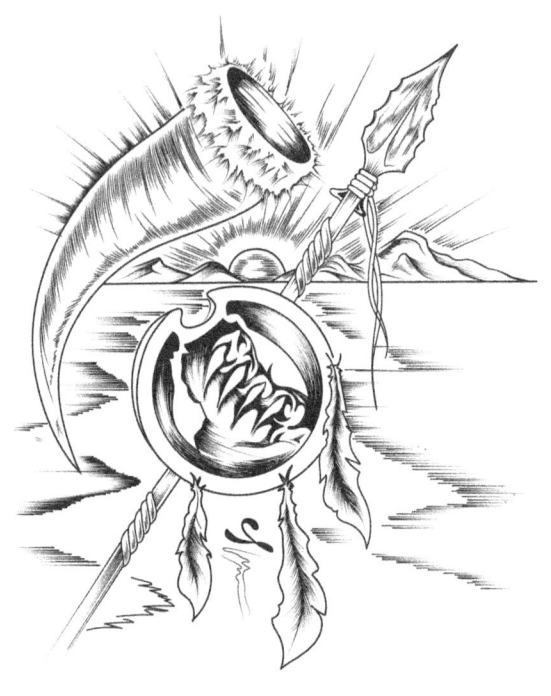

THEREFORE, TAKE UP THE FULL ARMOR OF GOD,

SO THAT YOU WILL BE ABLE TO RESIST IN THE EVIL DAY,

AND HAVING DONE EVERYTHING,

TO STAND FIRM.

— EPHESIANS 6:13

CHAPTER 4

FIGHTING THE SAME GIANT

I received severance pay when I resigned which lasted about sixty days. And, because I resigned on paper, I had no access to unemployment. Several things happened that fall of 2012. The first of note was that I had a Vision. More about that later. Shortly after the Vision, I argued with Paul again. I traveled to a well-known house of prayer for guidance and direction, and I began doing some contracted work. And, thanks to Paul and my own weakness, I had to battle a sexually transmitted disease. ***A Giant Shame.***

By December 2012, after taking a couple months off from working steady, I started looking for a job. It was then that I ran into JJ, whom I met a few years prior while working in the social service network for the homeless. By this time, JJ was the president of her own nonprofit counseling service. As I sat with her having coffee, she told me she wanted to give this counseling organization she'd created to me. She felt I was the right person to run it. I remember sitting there, thinking… it's odd that someone would be so eager to hand over a non-profit they created just because I was a good fit to be the president. I said—Let me pray about this first and get back to you.

I called JJ later and declined, but I offered to help as an independent consultant, and she accepted. I created a contract for services and helped obtain her organization's 501(c)(3) tax-exempt status with the IRS. I also assisted by writing letters, grant applications, and other support materials needed for administration, along with managing human resource issues that arose over the course of the next year and a half.

While I worked with JJ, I poured myself into trying to "fix" Paul. I convinced him to attend couples therapy sessions with me, working together in counseling with JJ. I agreed to walk alongside him and provide whatever was discovered in counseling that was needed to help make our relationship work. That was a really difficult task. What Paul was suffering from was not going to go away. It could only be managed, and only with the help of medication. But, we didn't even get that far. By the end of March 2013, I still didn't feel confidence in our relationship, even while doing the therapy. So I made the decision to not wear the promise ring Paul had given to me. I wanted to see real progress in the right direction before I made a lifetime commitment.

In the meantime, I cleaned the ring and placed it on a shelf. I looked at it all the time. I hoped and wished for things to move in a better way. Then one day, the ring disappeared. When I realized it was gone, I confronted Paul. He claimed he took it and threw it in the river because of a disagreement we'd had. I didn't believe him for one minute. Even though he was wasteful, it would not be like him to cast away something of such value. He had serious issues, and it would be more like him to sell the ring to get the money back for his own purposes.

When I think about all the ugly things I went through with him, I feel shame. I spent so many nights weeping and crying before I fell asleep. Where *was* he? I'd always known better than to be involved with him, but there was a deep desire in me for him. Maybe it was the beautiful things he created that kept bringing me back to him. But was what we had now the mud and muck that follows a tidal wave, the tidal wave I felt after we first kissed? Whatever it was, I was lovesick. He was like syrup. I went to great lengths to be with him to have a taste, even driving for miles and miles and miles.

But all that wasn't where his mind was. He wasn't able to move beyond the things that angered him in his childhood. The deception was too much to bear anymore. At the end of March, I kicked him out of my house. Again. That was the last time I saw him face to face.

Even after time had passed and I'd taken a job in a different area, Paul would call and attempt to manipulate me over the phone. When he found out I'd had a life-changing health crisis the summer of 2015, he called one last time and left a message saying he was sorry and that he would pray for me. He quit trying to talk to me after that. **Fighting the Same Giant face to face was over.**

CHAPTER

5

HOPE IN THE VALLEY

The Vision I'd had in the fall of 2012, after I'd left the ministerial Executive Director position, was set in a small town south of the Reservation. The town was insignificant other than that it supplied most of the Reservation's alcohol demands.

The small ministry I would occasionally visit as part of my job responsibilities was on the south end of that town. The couple who operated the ministry in 2012 lived on the property and I happened to meet them a few years prior. At the time we met they were inquiring about the ministry I was once a part of for nine years. They were seeking information about what it would take to run a homeless shelter. I recall sitting with them and praying for their needs. After that, I made a few trips to their ministry and we built a friendship.

When I visited them in the fall of 2012, I walked their property alone and received several things in the Spirit—*a Vision.* That day they were having their own Board of Directors meeting, and when they finished, they came out with one of their board members to greet me. I walked the property again, this time with them, and shared my vision. We entered a quonset hut and sat down together. While I laid hands on them, I prayed about the things I'd seen in the Vision along with whatever more Spirit now revealed to me. I saw the number "15,000" and an image of Native singers, dancers and drummers praising and worshiping the Lord.

That December of 2012, the same month I reconnected with JJ, I was praying at home and felt led to page through that day's newspaper. I came across announcements about fellowship grants from a well-known foundation. A light bulb came on! I researched the foundation and found the criteria for the grant application process, prayed, and began writing. The deadline was in three weeks. This was a perfect path to fulfill my Vision.

One of the requirements at the close of the foundation's fellowship was to design a sustainability plan for continuing the work. I wrote into the grant application my idea to build a nonprofit that would sustain the foundation's work and how that could be realized. I was excited!

I received a denial letter a couple months later, the same day Paul finally left. It was the end of March 2013, and I was disillusioned with the foundation's decision my grant proposal. I'd really felt the Lord had led me in this direction. I struggled with reconciling how I'd received so many things in the Spirit, and then the grant denial contradicted what I thought I'd received. Through much prayer, humility and surrender, I realized that I'd been trying make things happen by my own means. So, I figured the Lord would determine how it would happen in HIS way and in HIS timing. **Another Giant Battle.**

As time went on, I prayed about the Vision and the work I'd put into writing the grant. I remember thinking—I can't believe I put all that work into it and then nothing came from it. Then the thought hit me—Build the nonprofit anyway. You don't need a well-known foundation to fulfill the Vision!

I set a course to build the administrative structure for the nonprofit. For several months I searched for board members and wrote corporate documents: the vision, the mission statement, the corporate prayer, the purposes of the organization, and an outline for implementation. By the end of March 2014, my new team and I were ready to file documents to create the

501(c)(3) nonprofit.

Remember the executive director from a couple years ago? HE donated the money to pay the filing fee for my nonprofit! In October I received notification from the government that the corporation was an official tax-exempt nonprofit. **Hope in the Valley!**

CHAPTER

6

BATTLE AFTER BATTLE

It was up to me again. I felt it was ALWAYS up to me to charge forward and deal with difficult issues.

Dale was still my husband even though we'd been legally separated for five years. During that time he hadn't made a move to reconcile with me. He'd always struggled with managing money and waiting for him to pay for the inevitable divorce would be a long wait. So in May 2013, still unemployed, I scraped together $500 and filed for divorce. A judge signed the papers in July and my divorce was final. ***The Battle of Recompense.***

Throughout the many months that passed after I resigned, I applied for several jobs without results. I had increased my contract labor work and was applying for financial assistance for food stamps, utilities, and anything else I could find. Just before I was about to apply for food stamps, I received a piece of mail for my brother. He had used *my* address to file for financial assistance and had already collected the food stamp card that was for my benefit! I was furious. He didn't ask to use my address. He wasn't even living with me! The only legitimate source I had left to feed my son had been stolen by my own brother.

I became more and more desperate to make it from day to day. I figured if I tried to apply for food stamps during the same month my brother already had, I might be denied services. So I waited another month and then applied.

I found the journey interesting that God had laid out for me. I quickly saw the *other* side of the social service network that I'd worked with for so many years. When I filled out the initial paperwork, I was terrified. I was blindly handing over all my personal information and was afraid my identity could easily be stolen. I kind of closed my eyes when I gave my application packet to the clerk at the social services office. In order to receive benefits, I was required to show that I had been putting in applications for employment. And even though I had already been doing contract work, I was still required to attend a job class to be eligible for benefits. When I arrived at the class, I sat in a room full of people filling out forms, and I overheard their stories. On one hand were people desperate to take care of their children. On the other were those who were angry. They complained about the system and talked about how they would steal all they could from it.

When my turn came up, I was called to the front to visit with one of the benefit advisors. I informed him that I was doing contract work and asked him how that affected my situation. He explained the process for the self-employed: I would fill out a different kind of form to show the work I was doing and how much I was earning. I was so relieved that I wouldn't be required to provide evidence of job contacts I'd made in addition to sheets showing my contract work at the same time.

But by then I felt in my spirit that I wasn't going to find a job. I had already applied for over sixty: work I was qualified for, work I had experience for, and I even applied for entry level jobs. I got nothing. Whatever God was doing, it was looking more and more specific. I'd been working since I was fourteen. I *always* had a job and I always could get *another* job. Now He made sure every door was shut to me. I couldn't explain it to people, and I couldn't rescue myself.

I didn't have the answers but everybody wanted them. Some wanted to know what I was doing to fix my situation. It seemed no one understood, including faithful Christians I knew. This was some new work God was doing in me. I didn't understand and it seemed I wasn't receiving resolution from the Spirit. This troubled me.

For the first time, I encountered no one who had experienced this or had any similar reference point. No one was going to walk up to me and say: Yep, that happened to me, too. Here's what God's up to, and hang in there!

This was completely different from all I'd been taught in church and had studied. The very foundation of my understanding of how to walk in the New Testament promises of God was tumbling.

All I could do was try to survive. I found myself isolating more and more to avoid the beatings. The deeper and longer the Valley became, the more people tired of feeling compassion for me. They wanted a break from their conviction to help me. Relatives, friends . . . everyone closest to me all wanted to know: Why is this happening to you? You must be doing something wrong. Do you have a plan? You gotta have a plan. You must have made God mad for this to happen to you. Did you see that job in the paper? Well, did you apply for it? Why don't you go down the street and apply at the fast food joint? You must be too arrogant and proud. What are you going to do?!

Around the time my mortgage payment was sixty days

delinquent—for the first time—in May 2013, things in my house began to break. Paul had just left, and I had filed for divorce from my husband, but the judge hadn't signed off just yet.

The vacuum cleaner died, the dryer quit, door locks stopped working, water pipes began leaking. Things just broke, I had no money to fix them, and post traumatic stress disorder was settling in. Every time something happened I flinched. Loud sounds, normal changes in lighting, *everything* made me look over my shoulder. I remember saying to God—I am not getting it. I'm just getting PTSD, so how is this helping me, Lord?

I was overcome with deep feelings of inadequacy. I thought God had left me. I must not be holding up my end of the deal. I was going to miss out on something big because I wasn't getting it.

The second round of mortgage delinquency on my house came at the end of July. By then I was pleading with God to tell me what to do. There was a neverending wrestling match with self-condemnation…back and forthing with myself about my lack of wisdom…grasping for understanding of how God loves me. I found myself asking Him—Should I beg this time? Who should I beg from? Now that you have taught me humility, should I ask for charity from a church? A ministry? A person? Do I try to borrow money? Should I sell something? Are you bringing it this time, God? Am I supposed to fast this time, God? What is it I'm not getting, God?

That summer JJ was struggling, too. Desperate to rescue me with monetary support but not in a position to do so, she made promises to me that did not materialize. At the same time she criticized me, saying that I was not loving her enough. The additional spiritual warfare I encountered with JJ while we worked together was beyond difficult. I had to stay constantly grounded in order to manage such battles as this. I cried out to God— WHY?! It's bad enough that you have me going through this, but then I have to get hit on all sides from Christians, too?

One afternoon I sat in my house praying and laying hands on my own head, trying to pull the leaches off my spirit.

I'm amazed at humanity and of what we convince ourselves based solely on how we feel or think. We go to great lengths to attempt manipulating our environment to make it abide by the laws *we've* decided should govern our lives. We even twist the Word into what we think is right and wrong instead of believing the Truth of it. This was just as much Humanity's lesson as it was mine.

All these things took place the spring and summer of 2013. I found myself calling the very man who I felt had betrayed me: Tom. I was desperate, broke and needed help. He held the purse strings to the ministry I believed was the only resource that could help me. My pride was finally weakened and I was beginning to kneel in humility. I called him to ask for help, and he helped me with ministry dollars. I was so thankful for His saving grace. Now I could keep going.

I had three yard sales. I sold stuff right out of my house and through the newspaper. All the while I kept applying for jobs. The only one I was called back to a second interview for was with a school. It was 100 miles away but I pursued the job anyway because it was in the area where I felt the Vision would manifest. I wanted to put myself in that location and see what God would do.

I first interviewed at the school in August and made the second interview trip in September. During the second drive, the school's executive vice president called to let me know the power had gone out in the building where we were to meet. So there was no air conditioning, it was really hot in the building, and if I wanted to reschedule it would be okay with him. But I insisted on continuing…I was half way there already. My mom lent the gas money to me to make the trip and I didn't want to give up. If I gave up, I felt I would have wasted her money. I had to go. I was in a battle with the enemy and I had to keep going.

I had a great interview.

A close friend of mine has a remarkable gift for prophesying, and after the two interviews with the school she told me that she saw me getting the job. Even before the second interview, I had conversations with people and received a multitude of things in the Spirit, and read scripture that led me to believe I was getting this job.

The second week in September I was notified that I did *not* get the job. I was devastated. I felt like I'd literally lost my mind and I laid in bed weeping for two days. I felt deceived. Misled. I really needed that job. **Battle after battle in the Valley.**

Now, as I record this, I ask Him—How did I make it? *By my Hand*, He said.

CHAPTER 7

GIANT AFTER GIANT

Three weeks later, a massive, deadly winter storm hit. It began Friday afternoon on the 4th of October, 2013. We received more than five feet of snow in less than twelve hours. Forty thousand plus people were without power for more than a week. Thousands upon thousands of horses, cattle and other livestock were killed in the storm and lay dead in fields and ravines across the state. **Giant after Giant.**

I waded through deeper than waist high snow while it stormed that night, trying to save the young trees I'd planted in my yard. My dog, Sally, was out there with me, leaping up and then disappearing down in the deep and blowing snow. I became stuck in deep drifts on the side of my house and panicked. Oh my God! I'm not going to make it back into the house! I stopped. I was no longer on a fun adventure with my dog. Something in me kicked into survival mode. I worked my way backwards and finally back into the house, where I stayed until the storm passed.

A large tree in my back yard more than three feet in diameter snapped a limb and it fell on the power line to my house. For six days, everyone on my block had power but me. To this day my son and I tell stories about how I was going to flip out if I didn't get a hot cup of coffee! I sat at the kitchen table thinking—I can handle anything, Lord, if I only had a hot cup of coffee. While that simple pleasure became my primary mission for the next couple days, luke warm from the tap is what I got. I was grateful for it, and grateful for what food I did have. I remember savoring every bite because each meal might be my last. I found myself eating more slowly...reverently chewing my food. At this point all I could do was wait it out, survive.

Everything was blocked by the snow. Nobody was going anywhere, so hot coffee was out of the question for the first few days. One of my neighbors had access to heavy equipment and plowed out our street on days three and four. City plows weren't able to make it down our street for several more days. Then help arrived from out-of-state when electricians hooked up power to my house on day six. I sure was glad to see them. Another of my neighbors brought me a jar of homemade chili. **Blessings in the Storm!**

Little did I know that even more and bigger giants were another year and two away. But this one was clearly a turning point in the Valley that I didn't see coming. It seemed God intended to wear me out in order to accomplish His plan for me.

November was approaching and I continued to liquidate what I could to pay the mortgage. I tried borrowing money from the bank against the vehicle I owned but was denied because I didn't have enough income to make monthly loan payments. Without a job I couldn't even borrow money on something I owned! Selling the car wasn't an option; I would need it to get to the job I hoped to find. I became very angry and I dug out the papers for a small retirement pension I had been saving for fifteen years.

I could access only four thousand dollars from my pension fund, enough to cover the two house payments that I was behind plus a few other expenses. At forty-five years old, it pained me to pull *any* amount of money out. After accummulating debt years before when I was single and also during my marriage, I had changed my spending habits and learned to manage money. I worked SO hard to save this little bit for when I was older. Nothing was changing in my situation and there was no breakthrough finding a job.

I felt strongly that selling my house was not the God-given answer from my prayer time. I was afraid to explain that to anyone. I knew I'd get lynched if I revealed such a thing. When I asked God that specific question, what I got from Him was, *Take care of what I have given you.* He did not specifically tell me to sell my house, but I felt I had no choice. I had to try *something*. I had to put forth *some* sort of *different* effort. I decided to put my house on the market and began clearing it out at the recommendation of my realtor. By the end of November it was ready for sale. I was able to pick up a contract job, but interviews for a regular job didn't come until December. And the mortgage was sixty days delinquent. Again.

That December I interviewed on the Reservation for a position at a small school. During the drive over to the interview that morning I saw three eagles. Two were real and one was a carved wooden sign I saw just before I got to the interview location. I took this as a good omen and a confirmation that this was it. This is what I had been waiting for all this time. God had shut every door up till this point. The job would be on the Reservation where my Vision had taken place, or so I thought. I was hopeful.

✠

I felt the interview went well even though I didn't approve of the superintendent's behavior toward her Native colleagues sitting at the table. I was disturbed by the dynamics of their interactions. A week later I received what I felt was a misleading letter from the superintendent stating the Board of Directors decided to restructure the district and the position I interviewed for would not be filled. But within a week I saw the job reposted in the newspaper, which infuriated me. I wanted to write to the board members who were at my interview to expose the superintendent's falsehood. But I decided I didn't want to become a part of a situation with such lame leadership. I realized God was sending me to places in order to practice: reorganize, expose, shake the dirt off and set out in the right direction again.

Then my mind went into overdrive. I remembered part of a conversation I had with the superintendent who interviewed me. She happened to know Tom from a University class he taught. The recollection sent me reeling. I was consumed with the thought that he probably criticized me when she called him for an employment check. I couldn't get away from his control over other people! I thought I would have to leave the state if was going to find work.

It didn't matter. The mortgage was past due again and I didn't have the money to pay it. A week earlier my eldest sister told me by phone to let her know if I needed help. So I called her and asked for help with one month's worth of my mortgage payments, and I told her I would pay her back when I started working again. She came to my house and handed me a check to cover two payments. I cried. She cried. We cried. I was SO thankful. She didn't want to see me lose my house and was glad to help.

You need to know that this sister of mine is *the* most frugal member of my family. Handing me that much money was against her grain. In the past, if I ever said I was hungry before dinner, she would tell me to go drink a tall glass of water. So, when God moved her to do this for me, it was a shock. He is glorious! You just never know what God will do. **Victory in the Valley!**

CHAPTER

8

THE TESTING OF GIANTS

For those who are independent and self-sufficient like I prefer to be, this level of faith in God's promises was hard to grasp until it happens to me personally. Don't get me wrong, I had every confidence that God could move mountains, part the Red Sea and walk on water. People even commented on my confidence in Him (which I'd always attributed to God). If He says He's going to do something, it will be done. But now I was the one being tested by giants.

I still didn't understand what He was up to by taking me through this beating. Yes, I said beating. That's what it felt like.

That was the nature of my thoughts. Yep, God is kicking my butt. In my infinite wisdom, I would tell myself—You just got drop-kicked by God and there's nothing you can do about it.

Over the next several months I was in battle with a social service case worker. I had applied for child support several months earlier in the summer after filing for divorce. I really needed the financial help but it still hadn't arrived. I didn't understand it. My now ex-husband was employed and I saw no reason for the delay. After an agonizing fight with social services, the support finally began to come. **Another Battle.**

More months went by with no change in my employment, just battle after battle. It was hard to celebrate the victories that God DID give because I didn't have respite between battles to recuperate and reflect on what He was doing.

THERE WERE NO BREAKS, and that worried me. I felt myself becoming bitter because I was on edge all the time and I didn't like it one bit. I had been taught to reflect in the Word for revelation from the Spirit on what He was teaching me, then make the changes I needed to grow. I felt I was getting worse, not better.

I stayed in a routine as best as I could to be productive, including contract work, applying for jobs, and keeping the house tidy for possible buyers. I socialized very little because I just couldn't endure any more confrontations and mental anguish than what I already had.

CHAPTER

9

BREAKTHROUGH

My phone rang in March of 2014...more relatives asking if I there had been anyone interested in buying my house yet. No, I said. Then they questioned what my realtor was doing about it, and said they would be over to my house shortly to discuss this. My blood pressure shot up.

When they arrived, they had supplies for me they thought I should use to increase the appeal of my house. While we sat there at the table, they interrogated me again about what was being done to market my house and if I was doing everything I could to get it sold. I went on the defensive. I felt I had to defend what only God knew would happen next. Whatever His plan was, it wasn't good enough for them. I assured them I understood why they were upset. I said—You're not pissed off that my house hasn't sold yet. You're pissed that other people are helping me out. You think I should avoid being a burden to others. I continued—They don't *have* to help me, they *offered* to help me.

After reflecting on what I'd said, they replied: We don't understand why God has you going through this.

I said—He's not sleeping! He's aware of everything that's going on.

They wouldn't back off about what they thought I should be doing, and I wasn't backing off either. Now I began swearing at them!

They felt it was their right to express what they thought I should do. And, they felt they didn't deserve to be cussed out, and they got up and left.

I called them later but they didn't answer. So I left a voice message and apologized for swearing at them. We didn't talk again for two months. I knew they were upset. Not because of my situation, but because others were being sympathetic to me, and *that* made them envious. At this point in my journey I truly felt my name had changed to Job or Joseph. Good thing there was not a well hole in my backyard where they could throw me in! **Facing the Giants.**

Now it was May. One of my daily routines had become to drink coffee at my kitchen table and look through the newspaper for jobs. I came across a posting for the same job I had double-interviewed for back in August on the Reservation. Remember? The one I borrowed gas money from my mom to travel to. The one I lost my mind over because I misinterpreted my Vision. THAT one.

As I sat there, drinking my coffee, laboring over the paper, I asked the Holy Spirit—Well, do I even bother to apply? The thought came: *Well, you won't know unless you try.* I got on my computer and contacted the executive vice president about the position. He replied and he asked to set a time to visit over the phone.

When we had the phone meeting two days later, he offered the job to me and asked when I could start. I tried to remain calm! I let him know I would need at least two weeks until after Bradley got out of school to make the move. I started June 2, 2014. This was a major breakthrough in the front lines of the Giants. **Victory!**

I nearly lost my house at least four different times over the course of twenty-one months, from August of 2012 when

I lost my job until June of 2014 when God allowed me to work a regular full-time position with a salary. I was so relieved and thought the war was finally over. Nope.

CHAPTER 10

FALSE HOPE GIANT

With every new place there come new challenges. I found myself running a marathon, trying to keep up with new job expectations, trying to fit in, and building relationships with staff across the Reservation. I had to begin digging out of the Valley of debt, and my house was still on the market. Before I got the new job I had signed an extension with my realtor through the first part of July.

So every weekend I would drive back and forth to my house make sure everything was okay there, mow the yard or meet up with the realtor. It was nearly a two-hour drive one way and it was exhausting. And sometimes I made extra trips on weeknights after work, there and back in one evening.

It was June of 2014 and I'd been at my new job about a month. I got a call one evening from my realtor giving me a run down on an offer for my house. I told him I was going to take a day or so to think about it and check out the numbers he gave me. He insisted that I take the offer right then because no one else had shown interest in the house. I didn't like that he was pushing me, so I said I would call him right back.

I was nervous and sat down at the table. Something didn't feel right. I tried to think of a couple people to call and visit about the offer. But I didn't like the idea I'd come up with, so I began to pray. Who Lord? Who do I call? My nephew came to my mind. Great! I called my nephew and we visited about the numbers and the situation. He was a great help. He suggested I counteroffer and negotiate about the heating system before closing the sale. So that night I worked the numbers, figured out what I needed to swing it, called the realtor back and left a message for him.

The next afternoon while I was at work, my realtor called and left a message that the couple had withdrawn their offer altogether. Adrenaline shot through me. A False Hope Giant!

I was so shaken that after my contract with the realtor was up in July, I pulled the house off the market. I agonized about what to do next. Should I keep the house for a vacation home? I toyed with the idea all summer and then called my nephew again. He suggested renting it out and gave me the name of his property manager. I met with her and signed contracts that fall. I gutted the house, put some things in storage and my sister helped me haul the rest to my new job site where I was living in a rental.

My house went up for rent in December of 2014 and was occupied a few months later. ***Victory over the False Hope Giant!***

CHAPTER 11

KIDNAPPER GIANT

One of the first things I did when I arrived at my new job was enroll my son, Bradley, in the school where I was going to work. He was nervous about changing schools but he did really well. He played sports and I was so proud of him.

After Christmas, things changed for him. That winter and the next spring were a horrible time on the Reservation for everyone. There were more than sixteen deaths from suicide, most of them children. My son was overcome with suicidal thoughts, too.

I made arrangements for him to see a counselor once a

week after school that entire spring season. I hoped that if someone else was working with him besides me, that would help strengthen him. It didn't work. He still struggled, and I didn't even see small victories over his negative thoughts based on his strong foundation of faith and self-image. The only one the counseling seemed to help was me; it helped me cope with the things I had no control over.

I wanted to see him stand tall and go to battle against the enemy. I knew I wouldn't always be able to be at his side to guide him. No matter how much I tried to reinforce who he was in Christ from the scriptures and how much he was loved, he was losing the battle. He was a child. He didn't yet have the maturity and strength to battle what was happening to him. **The Giant who tried to Kidnap my son.**

There's NOTHING like hearing your sixteen-year-old son on the other end of the phone pleading for help because he's afraid he's going to hurt himself. You've never heard this voice before. It makes you stop in your tracks and come to the rescue in a panic.

I struggled spiritually—praying, laying hands on him, and weeping over him on many occasions. Then one time as I prayed in the middle of the night, wept and laid hands on him, he quietly said: Mom, I can feel water flowing through me.

Praise God! I can't tell you what took place in the Spirit that night, but now I had Hope. Later that spring as summer approached, Bradley's suicidal thoughts subsided.

I WAS THANKFUL.

CHAPTER

12

THE GIANT MIRACLE

Like I said, I'd run a marathon. It was June of 2015 now and I'd finally made it through the first year on my new job. I was exhausted. After my son was attacked spiritually, I asked
—What the hell am I doing here, God?

Part of my job was to deal with most major incidents that happened in the workplace. I remember calling one of my best friends and saying—You won't believe what's happened now! She got an earful that first year.

I'd been worried all spring about whether my contract

would be renewed by new my employer, and now it was the beginning summer. They did, but ... I actually hesitated to sign it. I didn't want to go back to the troubles of having no income again, but Bradley had been spiritually attacked here! I'd come to the Reservation on a fact-finding mission, to put myself in the place where I figured I would be doing ministry work for the next twenty years. Or so I thought. That first year had been a whirlwind and now I needed rest and I needed answers. I wanted to run to God and hide.

So I began making plans to spend a week up in the mountains by myself. I wanted to fast and pray and spend time alone with God. A friend who owned a cabin was willing to let me use it. We went back and forth on timing and settled on a date in late June, just a bit over two weeks away. I was excited about getting to be in a special place with my Lord.

On the Saturday afternoon before my upcoming retreat, my head hurt like I had a sinus headache. I tend to get sinus infections, so I figured I better get into the clinic. I remember the two-hour drive to the city with Bradley, looking over at him as I hunched over the steering wheel in pain. I said to him—This is why you need to learn how to dddrrrive.

After spending a couple hours in the clinic, they discovered my white cell count was high. They gave me a shot and told me to come back in the morning. My son and I stayed at my sister's house since mine was rented, and I went back to the clinic the next morning. They decided that since my body had responded to the previous day's medication, they gave me more of the same in pill form and sent me home. But that night I didn't feel much better and my head still hurt.

I went to work the entire next week. I made it through Thursday but I don't remember most of it. Like the prayer group I went to Wednesday night, or lunch I had with a co-worker on Thursday. It would take quite a long time for those memories to return to me.

Friday morning I was scheduled to drive with one of the nuns across the Reservation to see the other churches. As busy as I was, I was still looking forward to the drive. I hadn't yet seen all the locations under the umbrella organization I worked for. I was also to conduct a training that morning with some new summer volunteers.

I never made it.

CHAPTER 13

INTENSIVE CARE

JUNE 2015

I can't tell you the exact time it happened that Friday morning. I remember fragmented images and sensations of the things that happened. I recall looking at my good ol' flip phone and pushing speed dial to call my ex-husband. I remember feeling my body begin to die. And I remember dragging my body to the front door. I turned the lock, cracked open the door, and looked at the morning light in the sky. I distinctly remember thinking—I don't want the police to kick in my front door.

Memories of the next three to four weeks are of a nightmarish dream state mixed with flashing emergency lights and glimpses of relatives, friends and hospital staff. It was a good thing it happened before I headed off to be alone in my mountain retreat.

I am the youngest of four siblings. My mother and two older sisters, Laurene (the eldest), and Lynn (in the middle), made a hand-written account of what occurred during the next four weeks while I was in Intensive Care. Laurene is a registered nurse and happened to be visiting in the same town the day where I was airlifted. Some information was collected by friends and family afterward and added later. At times they made entries as if I wrote them myself *(shown in italics)*. I'd suffered a brain aneurysm.

JUNE 17 . . . . WEDNESDAY
LAURENE (eldest sister)

I was at prayer group tonight with Betty and Jean. She (Lisa) had complained to them that her neck hurt, and they prayed over her.

JUNE 18 — THURSDAY

MOM

Was at the doctor last Saturday. Can't get rid of the headache. Didn't realize something more serious was going on in my brain.

LAURENE

Last Saturday was seen at urgent care (thought I had a sinus infection). Blood work done–high white count–maybe an infection. Given a shot of Rocephin and sent home on Omnicef (antibiotics).

JUNE 19 — FRIDAY

MOM

Woke up, couldn't breathe. Got through to Dale and he called the ambulance to come and get me. Thought I was having an allergic reaction to the medicine for the sinus infection. Transported to local Reservation Hospital. Started tests, tried to walk and passed out. They did a brain scan and found a bleeding artery. Called larger city for a neurosurgeon. One was available, so they flew me in an air ambulance to major Hospital in big city. Kept me stable and tranquilized until Saturday morning. Laurene was already in big city visiting. She came and met the ambulance at the ER. Mom came over from across state, too.

LAURENE

That day I was in big city with my daughter to see the new baby (Jet). I got a phone call. Something was wrong with my sister Lisa and I should come home immediately. Nobody was able to tell me what was wrong, so I started packing to come home. Then I got a call back and they said to stay where I was; she's coming to me. I thought that didn't make any sense; there is a hospital where she's at already. What could she need that they couldn't do there? I found out she needed a neurosurgeon that could do coils (an endovascular treatment for intracranial aneurysms). I also talked with Dale later and he said you called him and told him "I'm dying" and were hysterical, so he called the ambulance.

LAURENE

Dr. S and Dr. B spoke with me about Lisa's treatment options. Dr. S said that where they have to put the coil would normally close off a portion of her brain. But God gave Lisa two arteries to the same place in her brain, and only one would be adversely affected. Dr. B put in a ventriculostomy to drain fluid from her brain to keep the pressure down.

JUNE 20 . . . . SATURDAY

MOM

approximately 7 a.m.

Taken to surgery to fix bleeding in the brain. Dr. S did the surgery; took a little over two hours. The surgery went very well. God gave me an extra vein to re-route the blood. **The Giant Miracle!** *Most people only have one and I had two—it's because of this I'm still alive. They put a little coil to block the bad one and re-routed to the other one. Everyone is praying it will heal well. Laurene, Mom and Aunt stayed at the hospital with me. I must* *remain in ICU for two weeks, room 3301. Two of my prayer group ladies came from the Reservation to pray for me (Betty and Jean). They prayed with me two times today.*

LAURENE

After the procedure I had to lay flat for six hours. Then the doctor's had respiratory therapist and RN remove the breathing tube. With the breathing tube out, I talked with my mom and Laurene. Had to be frequently reminded of what had happened to me.

JUNE 21 .... SUNDAY

MOM

Things are still pretty foggy. Lots of tubes in me. Laurene and Mom stayed in the afternoon with me in the hospital. Having a lot of head and neck pain. Doctor said it would last over a week. Jean and Betty came and prayed again Sunday morning and then they had to return to the Reservation.

JUNE 22 .... MONDAY

MOM

I feel a little better. Memory slowly coming back. Still lots of pain. Laurene had to go back to other city to work and will come back on Saturday, June 27. My brother's birthday is today. Mom stayed until 8:30 p.m.

LAURENE

In the morning I moved to room 3305 and was put on bi-pap ventilator because I was not getting enough oxygen.

JUNE 23 . . . . TUESDAY
MOM
9 a.m.

Mom is back at the hospital and stayed until 6:30 p.m. Left to have a soda pop with her uncle. Came back and stayed until 8:30 p.m. Having oxygen problems. They inserted right and left tubes into my chest cavity to drain fluid. Breathing better now because most of the fluid drained and left more room for my lungs. Left insertion was pretty painful, and I have to keep it in for two to three days until the fluid stops draining. Memory slowly progressing. Sisters, Stepdad and Uncle called to check on me.

JUNE 24. . . . . WEDNESDAY
MOM
9 a.m.

Mom is back at the hospital for the day. Slow progress. Memory lasting longer. Fluid drainage from brain getting lighter, a good sign. Lung cavity drains to remain in for a day or two longer. Talked to Cousin today. Also talked to Betty about prayer meeting tonight at employer's location. Lynn was going to come by with her son and Lisa's son Bradley, but she was unable to. Two ladies from the hospital came when Mom was at lunch and had me sign financial responsibility forms.* Numerous people checked on me today.

LAURENE

* Note: Lisa should not have been expected to sign financial responsibility paperwork with her traumatic brain injury.

JUNE 25 . . . . THURSDAY
MOM
8:30 a.m.

Not a good night. Lungs having a difficult time keeping up. Doctors decided to intubate again to help relieve stress on your system.

11:15 a.m.
MOM

Scheduled for a CT scan to check on brain spasms. They gave you more pain medications that helped. Slept most of the afternoon. Began to get more brain spasms so the doctor said they would go in again on Friday and put medication into the arteries to stop the spasms. Several people checked on you today.

LAURENE

Updating ex-husband Dale, Lynn, friend Betty and Brother-in-law on your progress daily. Every other day am keeping co-workers and your boss informed.

JUNE 26 . . . . FRIDAY
MOM
8:30 a.m.

Mom arrived at the hospital. Had a pretty good night but still having brain artery spasms. Scheduled for interventional radiology procedure after lunch at approximately 2 p.m.

Dr. S did the procedure. He used one of your groin arteries and went up to the brain arteries in the back of my head. He put medication there to keep the arteries open and not constricting. Only took about an hour. Did well.

Aunt came and stayed for about an hour. Everything went well. Doctor said it's possible they might have to do it again on Tuesday if the spasms come back.

Mom stayed until 8 p.m. The afternoon went well, and I am resting pretty good.

LAURENE

Spoke to the RNs and they stated that no medication was put into the brain. Wasn't needed after all. Dr. S was able to get a closer look at the arteries with the procedure than they could with testing.

JUNE 27 . . . . SATURDAY

MOM

9 a.m.

Mom arrived at the hospital. I did pretty good through the night. Slight agitation once around 9:30 a.m. A neurologist came by; says things are looking pretty good. Sometime in the afternoon they can take out the breathing tube.

Laurene is coming back today, and then Mom will go home, possibly until Wednesday, and then she will come back.

INTENSIVE CARE

LAURENE
1:30 p.m.
The doctor choose not to take the tube out of my airway until tomorrow. I remain on a Propofol drip for sedation.
4 p.m.
Still have the ventilator tube in. Woke up a little during the neurologist's recheck and Laurene reoriented me again.

JUNE 28 .... SUNDAY
LAURENE
8:30 a.m.
Laurene arrived and stayed with me until 10:30 a.m. While she was here, Doctor A neurologist came in and said I could have my airway tube removed. When Laurene came back at 12:30 p.m., the tube was out and I was able to talk, but weakly since my voice is hoarse after having the tube in my airway.

I'm pretty weak after laying in bed for several days. My head drain stopped putting out fluid in the early morning hours. The doctor states this is okay, and they won't do anything unless there are neurological changes.

LAURENE
7:30 p.m.
Lisa is very fatigued and I noticed some subtle neurological changes. She is okay for now.

JUNE 29 .... MONDAY

LAURENE

9 a.m.

I am still very weak and I remain extubated (without breathing assistance). Now I am on respiratory precautions because I have mycoplasma (a bacteria) in my lungs.

I had an episode with chest tightness. They did an EKG and gave me nitroglycerin. Then I felt better. I also had tachycardia today. Had a headache after the nitro.

10:30 a.m.

They took me off Dilaudid (strong pain medication) and I felt better. Theodore, my work colleague, came to visit and brought doughnuts, so Laurene ate them.

Mr. and Mrs. White (from church and ministry) came to visit and prayed over me.

I am coughing up phlegm and my throat is sore from that breathing tube.

2 p.m.

I was finally able to get up and sat in a chair until 3:30 p.m. Aunt is here visiting.

Laurene talked with the discharge planners about transferring me to the other city's Rehab Hospital upon discharge from here, so I can go home. I am still very forgetful.

8 p.m.

Lynn arrived to visit me.

JUNE 30 .... **TUESDAY**
LAURENE

8 a.m.

Laurene arrived and found me laying on my side. I have a headache and am very crabby.

10 a.m.

I left the floor and was taken to Interventional Radiology to check on my brain arteries. Dr. S. checked them again and this time he did put some medication (Verapamil) into my right PICA artery (one of three main arteries supplying blood to the brain) It was slightly narrowed. He thinks this will be the last time.

2 p.m.

When Laurene, Lynn and Aunt returned to my room after the procedure, I am still confused and crabby. I had to lay flat again for four hours.

LYNN (middle sister)

Lynn and Laurene went to visit Niece and baby Jet, and had lunch.

6 p.m.

Turned off the brain shunt (fluid was clear and very little drainage). Waking her up hourly to check her memory. (Laurene, this contributes to what is called ICU Psychosis.)

7 p.m.

Laurene left to return to other city.

8:30 p.m.

Lynn left for the night to stay at Cousin's house. Everyone is praying. Lisa wants to walk on the beach and have a drink of Pepsi or ice water.

JULY 1 ....WEDNESDAY
LYNN
8 a.m.

Lisa is on pain medications and doing okay. Very tired. Answering most questions correctly. We were able to sing praises. Ultrasound done. Dr. S says to do a CT scan. One-hour wake-up routine continues until 6 p.m. Dr. A says we are making good progress.

Speech therapy here at noon was mostly good but Lisa is not able to swallow yet. Dr. A says brain shunt will be removed tomorrow, and then she'll be awakened every two hours. Lisa still has a lung infection so we all wear masks.

2:30 p.m.

Chest tubes removed.

Mom, Stepdad and Aunt arrived. It was a little like the three stooges today. Very busy on the floor, plus we made a new arm band for Lisa. Lynn got her watch stuck in Lisa's hair. Twice. They put Lisa back in the wrong room after CT scan (just kidding). She asked for a fruit smoothie, a protein drink or orange juice.

INTENSIVE CARE   *71*

3:30 p.m.
 CT scan.

JULY 2 .... THURSDAY
MOM
8:30 a.m.

Mom and Stepdad met Lynn at the hospital. Stepdad and Lynn leave for other city about 9 a.m. Had more rain at home last night. Yesterday they took out the chest tube drain which helped reduce the pain. Eyes more clear today. Still slow progress (takes time to heal). Had a BM today; this is a good sign that her stomach is moving.

11 a.m.

Doctor A was here. Everything doing okay; may be having some spasms. Will probably take out temple shunt today.

12:45 p.m.

Dr. S came by and said you were doing good. Laurene talked to Dr. A when he was in your room. Aunt coming about 1:30 p.m. to see Lisa and Mom and then go to lunch.

JULY 3 .... FRIDAY
MOM
9:30 a.m.

Lisa was not allowed out of bed yet. We think the medicine is causing bodily distortion. Lisa was very clammy and sweaty for part of the day. Trying to help get her throat better; using swabs to make her strengthen her throat. She is still hoarse. Monitors stayed pretty good all day (oxygen, heart rate, and blood pressure).

1 p.m.

Aunt came for lunch and we watched the Zoo channel on TV with all the baby animals. They took out Lisa's head shunt today.

8 p.m.

Time to go to Aunt's house for bed.

JULY 4 .... SATURDAY
MOM
9 a.m.

Mom back again. Things were a little better at first. Late in the morning some problems with blood pressure.

10 a.m.

Dr. A came in and talked to Laurene by phone. Because of blood pressure problems, Lisa couldn't sit up in the chair yet. As the day went on, she got better.

Throat doing better but still can't have juice or jello yet. Later in the day, Lisa was feeling a little better and tried to sit up but was too weak. Will start tomorrow practicing getting up. Laurene and Mom to change places tomorrow.

JULY 5 .... **SUNDAY**
MOM
9 a.m.

Mom visiting for an hour and then Aunt picking up Mom for church with Niece and Nephew, and then be back about noon. You're doing better today. They sat you up for about 1½ hours in the chair. Vitals staying better today. Getting ibuprofen for pain and aches. Mom leaving at 2:30 p.m. to go back to other city. Laurene should be here about 8 p.m.

LAURENE

Lisa talked to her son Bradley on the phone.

7:30 p.m.

Laurene showed up and visited with me. We decided that this is a geographical oddity. We are two weeks from everywhere (family joke).

JULY 6 2015 .... **MONDAY**
LAURENE
9:30 a.m.

Laurene showed up. I'm still having a foggy memory. I was awakened at 2:30 a.m. by a tornado warning and was moved to the hallway. Now I am tired.

11 a.m.

Dr. R here to see me and to replace Drs. A and B. Dr. R states that the vasospasms are not gone yet, so we will continue with the same protocols until day twenty-one, which will be this Friday. She states it is not unusual to stay three weeks in the ICU.

2 p.m.

Aunt and Laurene are here. Aunt left at 3:30 p.m. Laurene and I visited a lot.

6 p.m.

I sat up in the chair for about an hour.

7:30 p.m.

Laurene is back from dinner. I am tired and slightly forgetful.

JULY 7 . . . . TUESDAY

LAURENE

9:30 a.m.

Laurene showed up. I had already been sitting up in the chair. Dr. R came in to see me and Laurene. Good news per Dr. R: the vasospasms have decreased so we can move to a step-down unit. Also, I no longer need the vasopressin drug IV so it was stopped, and then they took out the urinary catheter.

2 p.m.

I went by wheelchair to my swallow test.

3:30 p.m.

Back to my room.

LAURENE

Occupational therapist visiting me in my room. Per the RN and me, I flunked the test. My esophagus is too weak to swallow. I await speech therapy to explain what to do about it. I still have a feeding tube.

Report on swallowing: moderate problem in two areas. Both the oral (mouth) and pharyngeal (posterior) area of the tongue are not pushing food to the back. And weak posterior muscles are not swallowing. There is no aspiration.

JULY 8 .... WEDNESDAY

LAURENE

9:30 a.m.

Laurene arrived and I am sitting up in a chair. RN (Jewels) is in my room and washed my hair. Dr. R came in and stated I could definitely go to Rehab Hospital in other city on Monday (yay!). I sat up in the chair for three hours.

1:20 p.m.

Physical, occupational, and speech therapists came in to get me and I was gone for two hours.

They did a lot with me: practiced putting on pants, walked, tried to swallow different kinds of liquids, etc. When I got back to my room, Dr. D (a surgical resident) came to talk about surgery to place a PEG feeding tube in my stomach.

Dr. R says that Lisa needs it to be accepted at the other

Rehab Hospital and it will take four to six weeks for her to be able to swallow again.

4:45 p.m.

Lisa moved to room 3323.

6 p.m.

Lisa was scheduled for 11 a.m. tomorrow with Dr. B. Laurene left for other city.

JULY 9 .... THURSDAY
MOM

Aunt came in the morning and in the afternoon again to visit as both Laurene and Mom are in other city. Mom will be coming on Friday afternoon for the weekend, then take me to the Rehab Hospital on Monday. Closer to home!

Lisa is in room 3323 today and tonight. Did some PT today. Still having headaches in the night. Had surgery today to have the feeding tube put in her stomach. Slept most of the afternoon and was given pain medication because her stomach was pretty sore.

JULY 10 .... FRIDAY
MOM

Moved to fifth floor today and now I am in room 5163. Put an ice bag on my stomach since it was still sore. Aunt came about lunch time to visit for an hour.

Physical and respiratory therapists are here today, also. Mom got here about 5 p.m. and stayed until 8 p.m., then went to Aunt's house for the night. I'm having problems sleeping at night. My head still hurts.

JULY 11 . . . . SATURDAY
MOM

9 a.m.

Mom came to spend the day. I sat up in a big chair for a couple of hours. Went to physical therapy in the afternoon. Aunt came in the afternoon to visit for an hour. Mom stayed until 7:30 p.m. and then went to Aunt's for the evening. I am feeling a little better. Still can't swallow yet; I will work on that some more. I took my first shower and washed my hair myself for the first time in three weeks.

JULY 12 . . . . SUNDAY
MOM

9 a.m.

Mom and Aunt came for an hour, then they left for church where they saw Niece, Nephew and baby Jet. They have a good preacher at that church. Mom came back at 12:30 and stayed until 6:30 p.m., then went to see Cousin's new house. No PT today because it is Sunday. Stomach is feeling a little better. Only getting feeding tube and some pain medications now. Was able to take a shower again.

JULY 13 .... MONDAY

MOM

8 a.m.

Mom arrived. Lisa is getting discharged today to the other city Rehab Hospital. She complained of headaches last night and that the back of her head hurts. They gave her some pain medications and now she is feeling better. The physician's assistant for Dr. S came in and visited with Lisa. Waiting for discharge nurse.

LAURENE

4 p.m.

Lisa and Mom arrived at the other city Rehab Hospital and got checked in. Lisa is very tired from the long car ride across the state.

I HAVE NO PART

IN TAKING ON THE MIRACLE GIANT.

IT IS CHRIST ALONE.

CHAPTER

14

AGING GIANT

Three weeks later I woke up. What I mean is, I was more cognitive of what was going on around me. I remember laying in a hospital bed and my mother standing at the foot of it, looking at me, and telling me that I'd had a brain aneurysm. I remember feeling upset when I heard that.

I remember closing my eyes. Inside I cried out to God—Why did you leave me here?! Why didn't you just bring me home?! I could hear the voice of the Lord speaking. I couldn't make out what was being said or the conversation He was having with the other entity, but the words and the tone were

HIS; they were speaking in English. He turned toward me and said: *Rest*.

I calmed down. Then I realized my body had become hot and this emotional disruption made my head hurt even worse. When I reviewed the diary my family wrote while I was in intensive care, I deduced that this "conversation" must have taken place on July 4, 2015.

Before I could be released from the hospital to rehab, I had to achieve certain minimal activities. As I geared up to check out, I failed the swallow test. THAT was scary. If you've ever choked to the point you couldn't breathe, you have a good idea of what it's like to suffocate. Since I failed the test, they took me into surgery again, this time with sedation, to place a feeding peg tube in my stomach.

I was finally discharged July 13, wheelchair bound, on a LOT of medications, and had a long ways to go to real recovery. My mom drove six hours across the state that day to deliver me to the rehab center that was closer to both our homes. I made it, but the head pain I endured for the last hour of that road trip was beyond description.

The next couple weeks in rehab were also packed with pain. I had a strict routine with three different types of therapy, all of them three times each day. I thought it was quite interesting that God was showing yet another world to me, the world of how people interact with those they think are disabled or whose minds are gone.

Since I was assigned the status of NPO (nil per os, Latin meaning nothing through the mouth), I just stayed in my room to eat my water. It quickly became a joke and I told my sister, who happens to be a nurse, that NPO stands for No Public feeding Of animals. We laughed. But it did become irritating after awhile when some of the nurses caring for me continually asked what I wanted to eat from the menu. They'd forget I was NPO.

It wasn't until I was close to leaving rehab that I had another swallow test. This time I graduated to taking in small amounts of apple sauce, yogurt, toast and mashed potatoes. I was wheeled into the dining room where I sat with other rehab patients and listened to their stories. Everyone was at least fifteen years or more older than me and all had suffered strokes. I felt out of place, like I didn't belong there, and yet my brain injury qualified me and even made it imperative I be there.

When people came to visit me in rehab, they shared that they'd been praying for me, and some had even asked others to pray for me. I realized that thousands of people were praying for me. People I didn't even know were lifting me up. God showed me His greatness, His Great Love for me in the Valley.

☩

After I left the rehab center, I stayed with my mom for a few days, then moved back in to town to stay with my sister for a month which enabled me to attend outpatient therapies and followup doctor appointments.

Over the next thirty days I went from using a wheelchair to a walker, to a cane, to needing no support at all to walk. I continued to use wheelchairs for shopping for another two months while I built my endurance.

The more I healed, the more energy and hootspa I regained. I made verbal complaints to stores about their poorly designed floor plans and the lack of services for the physically disabled. I counted this yet another insight God granted me during my recovery. Apart from walking in others' shoes and deepening my compassion for those I once served, I wondered what it all meant.

On my last day in outpatient therapy, I watched the medical staff watching me. They were astonished to see me heal and go home so quickly. They could see that my God had done amazing things in me. But I didn't yet *feel* what they *saw*. It was only three months from when the brain aneurysm happened until I returned to work part time. In another thirty days I was back to full time. From the outside it appeared I was all better, but it would take another two years until my head wouldn't hurt for days after just bending over to clean or to lift a small box in my office.

One of the last outpatient therapies I received was shots in the nerves of my back to help reduce chronic pain I felt every evening. As difficult as the shots were to tolerate, they were worth it. Within a month, the pain from my nerves reawakening was gone.

Medications constantly changed as I continued to heal. The aneurysm sped up the menopausal process I had begun prior to it happening. My blood pressure was permanently changed, my physical endurance had left me, and I would be on aspirin for the rest of my life. I felt like I'd skipped years into my future, like I'd aged twenty years overnight. ***I was facing the Aging Giant.***

CHAPTER 15

SUICIDE GIANT

Now it was December of 2015 and six months had passed since the aneurysm. There were still a couple medical bills that the insurance company hadn't processed, so I called them to finally straighten out the situation. But their new security measures kept me from resolving the issue. I wasn't the insurance plan's cardholder.

I called my ex-husband, explained what was going on, and that he needed to call the insurance company. Eventually he was finally able to talk with a representative about the unprocessed claims. When he told them he was divorced, not just separated, they immediately pulled all my insurance coverage.

My ex-husband made several attempts to connect with his employer's main personnel department to verify what his local personnel staff had told him the previous spring. At that time, they insisted my coverage would continue even though we were divorced. But now, just a few months later, the main office told him it was his responsibility to notify them of the divorce by a certain date, which had passed. There was nothing they could do for me. All he could do was call me and apologize.

Needless to say, I flipped out. I can't even begin to explain the mental, emotional, physical and spiritual suffering I experienced. Over the next two months, every medical resource that had treated me after the aneurysm reissued invoices to me directly totaling more than $700,000.

I went through a four-week period with suicidal thoughts. I remember thinking—Why am I still here? Just put a bullet in my head! Why am I still alive for this, Lord? It's not bad enough that I died and came back, but now I have to go through THIS? I don't have the strength for this. I'm not even healed yet, Lord! All I heard was: *I will take care of this.* But those words didn't relieve my anguish. **Enduring the Suicide Giant.**

The suicidal clouds lifted about four weeks later, and

I haven't been able to correlate that shift to anything. God only knows.

During all that chaos, I still got up every morning and went to work. I called my employer's lawyer to ask for help. She gave me advice and referrals for additional legal assistance. One of the best things that was said to me during the chaos was, "You're going to get through this." That one thing gave me hope when nothing else did.

I spent the next several months stressed out and crying. To alleviate the medical debt, I had to pull myself together, write letters to those whom I owed money to, and apply for financial assistance programs from the hospitals. I wanted it all to go away, but it didn't. Nothing changed.

CHAPTER 16

BANKRUPTCY GIANT

Since it was not open enrollment season for health insurance where I worked at the time, I had to go outside into the open market if I wanted to get coverage. And, since I wasn't up to speed on insurance laws, I figured I'd also be penalized at tax time for not having insurance.

I visited with a bankruptcy judge to find out what my options were. It was clear I would lose or forfeit the majority of what I had left to my name *and* continue paying for many years to come. After the meeting I sat in my truck and cried, thinking about all the things I had already been through. Each and every day was a challenge, perpetually reviewing what I thought He had said to me, and what I believed I was supposed to hold on to during this journey.

Still, I kept getting up. That was the hardest part. I didn't *want* to get up. I was so tired of the laboring, of the doing. I didn't have a spouse to lean on. I was a single parent. No one was going to do it for me. God wasn't going to fill out the paperwork, write the letters and make the phone calls.

Already exhausted, I set about the task of pulling all my medical documents together and logged a detailed account of all events and conversations in order to apply for legal assistance. I headed out to see a lawyer that I was referred to, hoping to get help filing a possible insurance lawsuit. He asked for time to review my documentation and that he would get back to me in about three weeks.

Three weeks later I received a letter but it wasn't from the lawyer. It was from the hospital where I had surgery to repair my brain after the aneurysm. The letter stated I had been awarded 100% financial assistance. They wrote off the entire debt, which amounted to $600,000. *I couldn't believe it!*

I assumed the lawyer I spoke with must have written a letter to the hospital or called them. So I contacted him and he said: No, That is God! I didn't do anything. I thanked him for his assistance anyway and closed the case. I didn't have to file bankruptcy! **Victory! The Bankruptcy Giant was gone and His Promise prevailed.**

CHAPTER

17

LIGHT IN THE VALLEY

I made it to the one-year anniversary of my aneurysm: June 19, 2016. I wanted to really celebrate my Lord's victory over the bankruptcy giant with a huge banquet. But instead, I found myself feeling anxious. *Something* wasn't done.

By this time, my debts to the rest of the independent medical service providers had been sent to collections. If their bills weren't paid immediately, they went to collections automatically; the providers wouldn't wait for financial assistant programs to process my applications. Plus I was still waiting to hear if the Rehab Hospital's financial assistance program would discount or cancel any of those bills. My old mindset of lack of trust in Him interfered and I couldn't relax until it was all behind me.

This was the first full summer after my aneurysm and I quickly realized I couldn't tolerate the summer heat like I used to. Headaches came on easy and I had to seek out cooler surroundings. Just walking outside in the sunshine was a trial. I could only make it two laps around a track field before my head began to hurt and I had to stop.

One day I was sitting with colleagues from work, having a meal and listening to plans they were making for their summer months. Come to find out, they were going to conduct a music camp. That was perfectly aligned with the mission of the nonprofit I created: Support healing and revitalization of the Native people through music ministry. I was so excited that I could give some of my earnings to help fund sixteen kids who were enrolled to learn music that summer! I felt strongly that this was one of the reasons I was on the Reservation and what my income could or should be used to invest in. Hearing those kids play music after just one week of camp was worth giving the gift. ***A Light in the Valley!***

My attention on the dismal circumstances I faced lessened

and I felt inspired again. I felt the Holy Spirit really pushing me to write this book.

※

I went to a park one summer afternoon to write down some of my experiences. It was overwhelming. The emotions that welled up in me as I began to record events was too much. I said to the Lord—I can't do this. I feel like I'm being forced to relive it all over again instead of healing from the things I had lived through and learned from.

So, I made an outline of events but stopped there. It would be another two years before I picked up the pen again.

CHAPTER

18

COMING THROUGH THE OTHER SIDE

My son entered his senior year of high school in the fall season of 2016. I was so glad I was still here for him and get to watch him mature. We had many conversations about life and his need to continue on even if something else happened to me. He didn't like having these conversations but I felt compelled to tell him as much as I could about life and what I had learned along the way. We had a great rapport. If ever he felt I was giving him too much detail or was repeating myself, he had permission to tell me to stop monologuing and preaching. I tried to not irritate him too much.

In November, I finally heard from the Rehab Hospital's

financial assistance program. My application for help had been denied. The balance I owed went to collections immediately along with all the remaining bills for the smaller, independent medical providers. At the time, I understood the total to be $40,000 and *included* everything related to the Rehab Hospital. But later I found out that was not the case. Everyone who worked on me within the walls of the rehab center billed separately. The financial assistance program didn't apply to them.

My employer had previously offered to have a fundraiser to help me with unpaid medical bills. Back then I graciously declined because I thought I was covered by my ex-husband's insurance, but now I humbly asked for their help. They felt too much time had passed to ask for support from the staff, but the Board of Directors did approve some assistance for me. That enabled me to negotiate a reduced settlement payment to the Rehab Hospital that entailed putting a lean on my house and taking on a low interest loan for nine years. Those terms were a great deal better than the payment options I'd been facing so far.

That winter brought another surprising battle that ended in small claims court in the spring of 2017. I strongly felt the

Holy Spirit pushing me to stand my ground on certain medical debts in a way that delayed settling the claims for awhile. In the meantime, my truck had broken down. As it turned out, the money I needed to fix my truck was provided at just the right time because going to court kept money in my pocket a little longer. Go figure. If I had settled the case earlier, I wouldn't have had the money to fix my truck.

☒

While all that was happening, I faced yet another tribulation, this time with my son. He decided he wanted to enlist in the military. I was very concerned but didn't want to spoil his momentous leap into adulthood.

You need to know my son was diagnosed with Asperger Syndrome at the age of five. I worked with him for many years, answering all of his why questions and bridging social gaps. I couldn't predict how a military experience would affect his mental state, but I was pretty sure the intensity of basic training and other new demands would pull him backward instead of propeling him forward.

To his credit, though, he'd made leaps and bounds as he was growing up and overcame things I wasn't sure he could. He played sports and did great. So, I thought maybe, just maybe, if he went to a few drills and got a feel for it, maybe he'd make the transition to the military successfully.

Well, that didn't happen. He began cutting himself because

he didn't know how to express his desire to change what was happening. I was able to help him recognize his feelings, and then he was able to make the call himself. Luckily it was early enough in the enlistment process that he could withdraw.

I can't begin to explain the negativity this brought out of family and friends who are veterans or military supporters. Just trying to buffer my son from their reactions was ***A Giant Undertaking.***

You just never know what the will of the Father is going to look like.

In the spring of 2017, I lost in small claims court but was afforded the opportunity to continue making payments for awhile. The only way I could avoid a wage garnishment was to give the creditor permission to make automatic withdrawals from my checking account. I don't trust that kinda stuff one bit. But I went ahead and authorized it to buy a little more time to figure out how God wanted me to settle the $6,000 balance.

It was now May of 2017 and my son graduated from high school. HALLELUJAH! What a great day. I was so thankful to witness his graduation. ***A Victory in the Valley!***

CHAPTER

19

GIFTS FROM ABOVE

Taking back my house after renting it out for two years was a difficult decision but one I felt strongly about. The longer I continued renting it, the more damage it would likely sustain. At this point I thought it would be nice to give it to my son if something should happen to me again. We discussed it on a couple occasions and I made suggestions for things he could do with the house to supplement his income as he got older or if he wanted to move away.

It was summer again and the second anniversary of my aneurysm came around. The nun whom I was supposed to travel with that fateful day in 2015 had not yet left for the summer this year, so we decided to celebrate together with lunch at the local casino. I thanked the Lord for giving me another year.

When I took back my house, I lost the income from the rental. At the same time, because my son had graduated from high school, the child support he had been receiving from his father ended. I needed to somehow lower my monthly expenses. I wrestled with the idea of moving completely back into my house instead of living there part time and then part time on location at my job. It would eliminate the extra rent I was paying for two houses, but that really wouldn't resolve my financial problems. I would be adding expenses from living in my own house again, plus incurring many more long distance trips every week back and forth to work. That would take a toll on my pocketbook and my health, but I needed to do something.

When I asked God if I should move back into my house full time, all I heard was: *Stay*. I struggled with this message because I couldn't see past my circumstances. It seemed logical to me to eliminate paying rent near my workplace, but God kept saying: *Stay*.

So, I set out to visit the bank to see if I could get the mortgage insurance removed from the loan on my house. That didn't fly with them. I had a nice conversation with the loan officer, but I still needed to pay off another $5,000 of the principal amount to get rid of the PMI. I didn't have it.

Defeat. Again.

Then, out of the blue, I received a letter in the mail from the city saying that the flood zoning had changed in my area and I was no longer required to carry flood insurance. The flood insurance more than doubled my homeowner's insurance, so this was a huge blessing from the Lord! But then another battle came. The insurance company made it as difficult as possible to remove the flood coverage from my policy. I had to jump through their hoops to prove the city's new zoning policy even though it was printed in the local paper for all to see. Finally, a month later, I was rid of it. ***Victory over the Insurance Giant!***

And then, out of nowhere, I received a notice from the lender the following month that PMI was no longer required for my home loan. My mortgage payment would drop even lower. **Another Victory Gift from the Lord!**

TRUST IN THE LORD WITH ALL YOUR HEART,
AND DO NOT LEAN ON YOUR OWN UNDERSTANDING.
IN ALL YOUR WAYS ACKNOWLEDGE HIM,
AND HE WILL MAKE YOUR PATHS STRAIGHT.

— PROVERBS 3: 5-6

CHAPTER 20

REBUILDING THE FOUNDATION

Previously I viewed life's battles as declarations of spiritual warfare, and that it was my job as a prayer warrior to engage in the battles to bring down the enemy. Now I look at the battles differently.

Now I see that *everything* comes from God's hands. Not that I think I have His sovereign authority, but I feel God's omnipresence in all things. Now I know God doesn't *cause* bad and difficult things to happen, and nothing happens without His knowledge. He uses all things for His own purpose: that we should become closer to Him. Can you believe it?!

We can't get closer to Him if we're not of the same mind, even when we think we've achieved some sort of spiritual enlightenment or think we're living out the measure of faith bestowed upon us. Whatever portion He has allotted us, He always wants to increase it. Why? Because He loves us that much. HE loves ME that much. He loves YOU that much. I finally feel it throughout everything. He wants to be with us.

Trusting Him is what my journey through the valley of the giants was all about. HE, not I, must be the one to remove obstacles and hindrances that prevent me from receiving His love and understanding.

> ...SO SHALL MY WORD BE THAT GOETH FORTH OUT OF MY MOUTH: IT SHALL NOT RETURN UNTO ME VOID, BUT IT SHALL ACCOMPLISH THAT WHICH I PLEASE, AND IT SHALL PROSPER IN THE THING WHERETO I SENT IT.
>
> — ISAIAH 55:11

To accomplish His will, He takes us through experiences that challenge our unbelief—or, more appropriately—our false beliefs.

Do you have unbelief encamped somewhere in you? Do you rely on your own abilities and understanding to save yourself? Do you try to get yourself out of the pits you get into?

You might think philosophically that you're certain of who God is, that He is your Savior. And you may insist your faith is strong. It's a good thing He loves you so much that He won't abandon you there in your false belief. He will make you face the grave mistake of leaning on your own understanding.

> I WILL NOT LEAVE YOU AS ORPHANS;
> I WILL COME TO YOU.
>
> — JOHN 14:18

In order to increase your faith, God guides you through the emotions and thoughts that seeds of unbelief have planted in you. His guidance comes only when you surrender and take the time to reflect on who you really are in Christ.

He's not trying to hurt you. He wants to expose your false beliefs, to bring them up from the depths of your mind to the surface. Only He knows what you must experience. You're in His hands. He is the Potter and we are His clay. When I asked

Him if I was truly in His hands, He said: *You are in my Heart.*

There are so many scriptures and parables that support my experience. Some call it pruning, cleansing, walking through the fire or through the valley of the shadow of death. I've even heard it called surgery. Some of your life experience may feel like what Joseph's brothers did to him. I felt like I didn't have God's favor. I call it my *Journey Through the Valley of the Giants*. The more I tried to save myself, the bigger and more overwhelming everything became. So much so I couldn't figure out what to do on my own, and He made it so. Whatever you want to call it, regardless of your doctrinal background, it can be very painful but is always very worth it. Knowing Him is very worth it! **He is worth it.**

FOR IT WAS FITTING FOR HIM,
FOR WHOM ARE ALL THINGS, AND THROUGH WHOM
ARE ALL THINGS, IN BRINGING MANY SONS TO GLORY,
TO PERFECT THE AUTHOR OF THEIR SALVATION
THROUGH SUFFERINGS.

—HEBREWS 2:10

epilogue

THE JOURNEY CONTINUES

After finishing the written manuscript for *Journey Through the Valley of the Giants,* I connected with a writer who was inspired by my story and wanted to help publish it. Within two months he was diagnosed with cancer and passed away just nine months later. Since then, both my vehicles were destroyed in a hail storm (and I didn't have insurance to recover from the losses.) I've undergone eye surgery and one of my lungs collapsed—three times—requiring two lung surgeries. The winding road to publishing this book took another disappointing turn, but the path u-turned and now you're holding this book! Then, a virus our world had never seen before, COVID-19, became a global pandemic. **Living With Giants...**

about the author

L. J. LONG

L.J. Long, nom de plume (pen name), has been a Christian for more than 25 years and worked in faith-based nonprofits for 15 years, serving as a board member for several of them. She is trained in Biblical Counseling and Critical Incident Stress Management. At the beginning of her 5-year season of journeying through the valley of the giants, the Holy Spirit moved Long to behold a vision which inspired the organization, development and creation of a 501(c)(3) nonprofit named 7 Rivers Revitalization Group, Inc. The vision was a catalyst and roadmap for the path she would walk through the valley of the giants . . . and beyond.

To contact the author,
please send an email to Journeywithljlong@gmail.com
or visit www.lisajlong.net

www.ingramcontent.com/pod-product-compliance
Lightning Source LLC
Chambersburg PA
CBHW071355080526
44587CB00017B/3113